There is a tree ir

There is a hole in the tree.

There is a squirrel in the hole.

What shall I have for breakfast?
Empty
I know.

Chocolate.

I love chocolate.

Where has it gone?
CHOCOLATE

I love chocolate.
So do I.
Pesky birds.

I know.

I hid an apple here
last week.

Sparrows
pond
way out
Castle
Where is it?

I love apples.
So do I.
Pesky birds.

I know.

Playground
Bridge
Garden

Good. I'm
just in time.

Billy Steel

Here goes.

I like nuts.

Yum, yum.

In the park ...

I know.
What?
We can go to the garden and eat some nuts.
I like nuts.
So do I.

Where have they gone?

I like nuts.